AMERICAN PLACES

From Vision to Reality

One World Trade Center

by Meish Goldish

Consultant: Eric Darton, Adjunct Faculty
New York University Urban Design and Architecture Studies Program
New York, New York
Author of *Divided We Stand: A Biography of the World Trade Center*

BEARPORT PUBLISHING

New York, New York

Credits

Cover, © alredosaz/Shutterstock; TOC, © Felix Lipov/Shutterstock; 4, © Sean Adair/Reuters; 5L, © 615 collection/Alamy; 5R, © Eric J. Tilford UPI Photo Service/Newscom; 6T, © POOL/REUTERS/Newscom; 6B, © FEMA/Alamy; 7, © Vanbeets/iStock; 8, © Keith Bedford/The New York Times/Redux; 9L, © Archimation UPI Photo Service/Newscom; 9R, © Terese Loeb Kreuzer/Alamy; 10, © ZUMA Press, Inc./Alamy; 11, © Chip East/Reuters; 12, © Joe Woolhead/SIPA/Newscom; 13L, © VINCENT LAFORET/Redux; 13R, © Lucas Jackson/Reuters; 14, © Richard Levine/Alamy; 15L, © Oliver Multhaup/AP Images; 15R, © Mark Lennihan/AP Images; 16—17, © SIPA USA/SIPA/Newscom; 17R, © Mark Lennihan/AP Images; 18, © Joe Woolhead/Sipa USA/Newscom; 19, © Justin Lane/EPA/Redux; 20, © Michael Doolittle/Alamy; 21L, © RomanSlavik.com/Shutterstock; 21R, © kev303/iStock; 22L, © Dorothy Alexander/Alamy; 22R, © Joe Woolhead; 23, © Steve Spak; 24L, © Joseph Reid/Alamy; 24R, © Allan Tannenbaum/Polaris/Newscom; 25, © Dibrova/Shutterstock; 26L, © Christopher Penler/Alamy; 26R, © Glynnis Jones/Shutterstock; 27T, © Jgorzynik/Dreamstime; 27B, © Michael Matthews/Alamy; 28, © Digitalfarmer/Alamy; 29, © cate_89/Shutterstock; 31, © meunierd/Shutterstock; 32, © Ritu Manoj Jethani/Shutterstock.

Publisher: Kenn Goin
Senior Editor: Joyce Tavolacci
Creative Director: Spencer Brinker
Design: The Design Lab
Photo Researcher: Thomas Persano

Library of Congress Cataloging-in-Publication Data in process at time of publication (2018)
Library of Congress Control Number: 2017039205
ISBN-13: 978-1-68402-435-3 (library binding)

For more information, write to Bearport Publishing Company, Inc., 45 West 21st Street, Suite 3B, New York, New York 10010.
Printed in the United States of America.

10 9 8 7 6 5 4 3 2 1

Contents

Fallen Towers

On September 11, 2001, **terrorists** crashed two airplanes into the twin towers of the World Trade Center in New York City. Fuel from the planes caused fiery explosions, and both of the 110-story skyscrapers were soon **engulfed** in flames. Less than two hours later, the buildings **collapsed** in a pile of smoky rubble. More than 2,750 people were killed.

When the twin towers were built in the early 1970s, they were the two tallest buildings in the world. Each stood more than 1,350 feet (411 m) high.

Americans across the country were shocked by the attacks and the terrible destruction. People wondered what would happen next. In a speech to Congress two weeks later, President George W. Bush promised, "We will rebuild New York City." Yet how, exactly, would that be done?

President George W. Bush

Several smaller buildings at the World Trade Center site were also badly damaged in the attacks.

Different Views

Rebuilding the World Trade Center would be a difficult job—and there were lots of opinions about how it should be done. Some people felt that nothing should be built on the land where the towers fell. They argued that it was "**hallowed** ground," since many victims' remains were never found and stayed buried in the earth.

Workers spent more than eight months searching for victims' remains and cleaning up the World Trade Center site after the attacks.

Workers had to clear away piles of twisted steel and broken glass at the site.

Other people wanted a **memorial** built on the site to honor the victims of the 9/11 attacks. Still others felt that it was important to rebuild the World Trade Center, with one or more skyscrapers. Doing so, they believed, would show that America's spirit hadn't been broken by the attacks. Was there a way to satisfy everyone?

Some people wanted the World Trade Center to be rebuilt exactly the way it was before the 2001 attacks.

The Contest

Shortly after 9/11, a group called the Lower Manhattan Development **Corporation** (LMDC) was formed. The group was in charge of rebuilding the area destroyed in the attacks. In 2002, the LMDC decided to hold a contest. They invited **architects** and designers from around the world to send in ideas for the site. More than 13,000 people from 94 nations responded. The public was then invited to comment on the entries.

New York State Governor George Pataki (center right) and members of the LMDC tour the site.

The LMDC included 16 members who were selected by Governor George Pataki and New York City Mayor Rudolph Giuliani.

After a long **debate**, an architect named Daniel Libeskind was chosen as the winner. The LMDC liked his idea best because it included both a memorial to honor the victims plus an office tower with an unusual design. Libeskind wanted the skyscraper to be 1,776 feet (541 m) tall, in celebration of the year when the United States declared itself a free nation. New York State Governor George Pataki named Libeskind's building the "Freedom Tower."

Daniel Libeskind said he wanted to create "a space for people, not just corporations."

Libeskind's winning design

A Slow Start

New York City now had a plan for rebuilding the World Trade Center. However, several years passed before construction of the tower began. During that time, there was much arguing among city and state **officials**, building owners, and construction companies. Each of them had a say in how the nearly four-billion-dollar project would be carried out.

In a ceremony held on July 4, 2004, workers laid the **cornerstone** of the Freedom Tower. However, it would take nearly two more years of planning before the actual building of the tower could begin.

Complicating matters, the site's **developer**, Larry Silverstein, didn't like Libeskind's design for the tower. Because Silverstein held the **lease** to the site, he had the power to choose his own architect. He picked David Childs as the lead architect, and Libeskind was named master planner. Together, the two men worked on the skyscraper's final design, which included a shiny **geometric** exterior and a long **antenna**.

In 2005, architect David Childs (left) showed his model of the Freedom Tower to Governor George Pataki (center) and developer Larry Silverstein (right).

Digging Deep

In April 2006, construction of the Freedom Tower finally began. First, workers dug a huge hole in the ground nearly 200 feet (61 m) deep. It reached all the way down to the thick, solid bedrock that lay far beneath the soil. The gigantic hole would serve as the base of the skyscraper.

Construction teams worked day and night to dig a base for the huge building.

The earliest digging had to be done by hand. Why? The site was near a subway station. If workers used **dynamite** or heavy machines to loosen the soil, they might cause damage to the station. Instead, workers used simple digging tools. "You had people down there with picks and shovels, maybe digging a foot a night," said Dan Tishman, the head of the construction company managing the site.

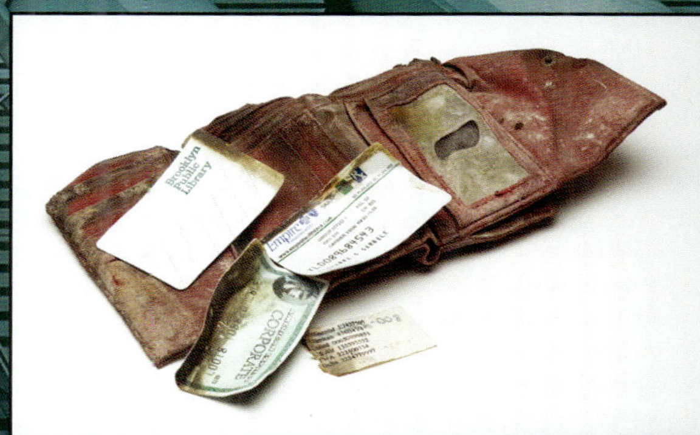

As construction workers dug deep, they found the belongings of some 9/11 victims. There were keys, wallets, and other personal items.

While digging in the earth, workers discovered part of a boat from the 1700s that had been buried in an old **landfill**!

Filling the Hole

By November 2006, workers had finished digging the hole that would help form the skyscraper's **foundation**. It was as tall as a 19-story building—only underground! Then, 40 large trucks poured nearly 81,000 gallons (306,618 l) of **concrete** into the hole to create a super-strong foundation.

Trucks poured concrete to form the building's giant foundation.

Meanwhile, high-strength steel beams that would be used to support the building were being made overseas in Luxembourg. This tiny European country is home to a factory that specializes in making the heaviest steel beams in the world. The beams, called "Jumbo Sections," would each weigh 70 tons (64 mt)! After months of work, the steel beams were finished. Then, they were shipped to New York City, where workers planted them upright around the **perimeter** of the foundation.

A worker inspects a Jumbo Section.

The beams and concrete had to be strong enough to support the entire weight of the tower—48,000 tons (43,545 mt). That's about as heavy as 6,200 elephants!

The public was invited to sign the first beam before it was planted into the skyscraper's base.

Floor by Floor

After working for more than two years on the tower's base, workers were ready to start building up, floor by floor. The job began with ironworkers, who connected **vertical** beams to **horizontal** beams to create a frame for each floor. The work was incredibly hard. "The entire day is a struggle. Every muscle aches," said Michael O'Reilly, an ironworker.

The frame for the skyscraper was built with steel beams, one floor at a time. It took about a week to complete each floor.

The ironworkers worked together in teams. First, a raising gang used cranes to lift the steel beams into the air. Then, signalmen guided the beams toward other workers called connectors. While carefully balancing on the narrow beams, these men bolted the beams together. One wrong move could send a worker tumbling to the hard ground below. Ironworker Thomas Hickey said, "You really put your life on the line every day."

Strong winds often made the building beams shake. Sometimes a worker would lie down on a beam less than one foot (30 cm) wide in order not to fall!

The frame of a building, like the skeleton of a human body, holds the entire **structure** together.

Hot and Cold

Staying balanced on the beams wasn't the only challenge for ironworkers building the tower's frame. The changing seasons and weather also caused problems. In the blazing summer sun, the steel beams grew so hot they could burn a worker's skin. Ironworkers wore gloves and other thick clothing for protection as they pushed the beams into place.

Workers atop hot steel beams

Freezing temperatures also created problems for the workers. "Winters really put a beating on you," said Jorge Fernandez, an assistant **foreman** at the site. "But we have a saying: 'The heat's in the tools.' The more you work, the less cold you'll be." As the building slowly inched closer to the sky, the ironworkers enjoyed a view that hadn't been seen since the day the twin towers fell.

The unfinished skyscraper survived the heavy winds and rain brought by Hurricane Sandy in October 2012.

When Hurricane Sandy struck New York City in 2012, much of the ground at the tower became flooded. Luckily, the building avoided serious damage. Less than a week after the storm, workers were back on the job.

The Finishing Touches

After the frame for each floor of the skyscraper was completed, other **tradesmen** joined the team. For example, carpenters **installed** floors, walls, ceilings, and doors. Electricians laid electrical wires, and plumbers put in pipes.

Thousands of people worked together to build the tower.

Other workers attached large glass window **panels** to the outside of the building. However, strong winds often caused problems during the installation. "These gigantic panels act like a sail," explained Robyn Ryan, a manager for the window installers. The workers used wires to help control the movement of the panels on windy days. "But if the wind is too high, it's just too dangerous," said Ryan.

Workers attached 12,774 glass panels to the outside of the building.

Each glass panel is 13 feet (4 m) high and 5 feet (1.5 m) wide and weighs about 1,200 pounds (544 kg).

The tower used enough concrete to make a sidewalk that would stretch all the way from New York City to Chicago.

Keeping Safe

Safety was always a main concern for workers at the skyscraper. Even before the tower was built, a 40-foot (12 m) high model of the building was constructed. It had 24 glass panels attached to the outside. The model was thoroughly tested to make sure the concrete and glass could remain standing even in a powerful earthquake.

Safety netting (shown in blue) was put up to prevent workers from accidentally falling off the building.

Workers wear safety harnesses as they dangle from a crane.

In 2009, city officials decided to change the name of the tower to One World Trade Center. However, people still take pride in remembering and using the earlier name, "Freedom Tower."

Protection from a possible terrorist attack was another concern. All the concrete walls in the stairways and elevator **shafts** were made 3 feet (91 cm) thick, so the skyscraper could stand strong if a bomb went off. Air **filters** were placed inside the building in case of a poison gas attack.

The building's deep base was filled with concrete so it could withstand a powerful explosion.

At the Top

By the end of 2012, One World Trade Center was nearly completed. The last job was to attach a 408-foot (124 m) **spire** to the top of the 104-story tower. The spire was built in Canada in 18 large sections. Then the sections were shipped by boat to New York City. Some sections weighed as much as 67 tons (61 mt) each.

Workers used cranes to bring the pieces of the spire up to the skyscraper's rooftop.

Trucks drove the sections of the spire through the city's streets in the middle of the night to the building site. Giant cranes lifted each section to the roof. Then workers spent months connecting the 18 huge pieces. On May 10, 2013, the final section was set in place. The spire made One World Trade Center 1,776 feet (541 m) tall—the tallest skyscraper in the **Western Hemisphere**!

President Barack Obama signed a steel beam that was placed at the top of One World Trade Center. In red marker, he wrote: "We remember. We rebuild. We come back stronger!"

Remembering Heroes

The finished One World Trade Center soars into the sky and is a **beacon** of hope for New Yorkers and many others. However, it's not the only standout structure at the World Trade Center site. The 16-acre (6.5 ha) area also includes a 9/11 museum and memorial. The museum displays items from the attacks, including damaged fire trucks and twisted steel from the collapsed towers.

One World Trade Center has a three-story observation deck on floors 100 to 102.

A large statue called "America's Response Monument" stands in front of One World Trade Center. The statue honors Americans who fought in the war in Afghanistan after 9/11.

The memorial includes two giant, sunken pools of water. They are located in the exact spots where the twin towers once stood. Magnificent waterfalls run down the sides of each pool. The names of all the 9/11 victims are **etched** into the low bronze walls surrounding the pools. The memorial serves to remind people of the attacks and to honor those who tragically lost their lives that day. In President Barack Obama's words, "We remember. We rebuild. We come back stronger!"

One of the memorial pools

Visitors can read the names of all the 9/11 victims at the site.

One World Trade Center

BY THE NUMBERS

Height of Lobby Ceiling:
55 feet (17 m)

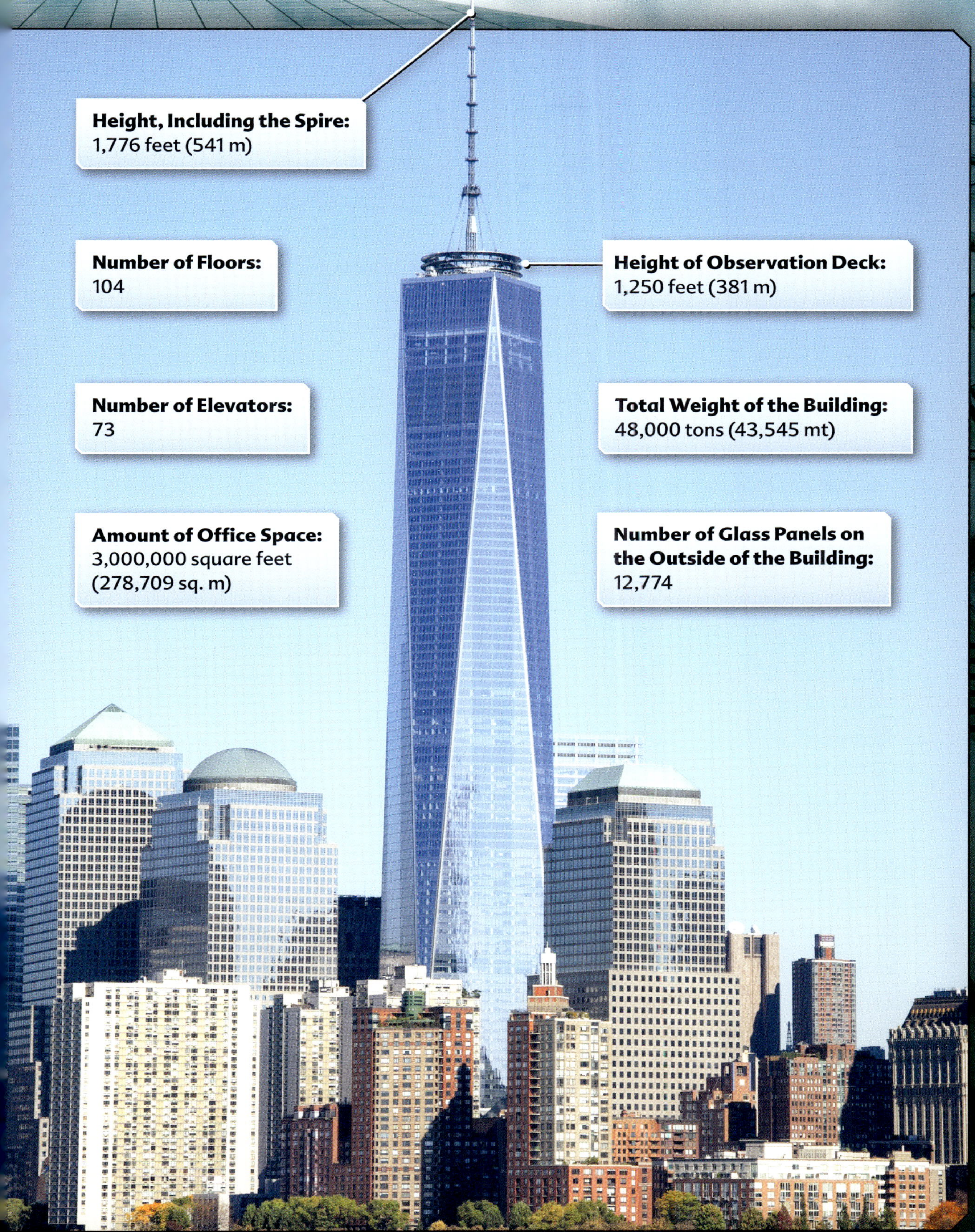
Height, Including the Spire:
1,776 feet (541 m)
Number of Floors:
104
Height of Observation Deck:
1,250 feet (381 m)
Number of Elevators:
73
Total Weight of the Building:
48,000 tons (43,545 mt)
Amount of Office Space:
3,000,000 square feet
(278,709 sq. m)
Number of Glass Panels on
the Outside of the Building:
12,774

Glossary

antenna (an-TEN-uh) a long rod or wire used to transmit signals

architects (AR-ki-tekts) people who design buildings

beacon (BEE-kuhn) a signal

collapsed (kuh-LAPSD) fell suddenly to the ground

concrete (kon-KREET) a mixture of sand, water, cement, and gravel

cornerstone (KOR-nur-stone) a special stone set at the corner of a building

corporation (kor-puh-RAY-shuhn) a group of people who are allowed to run a company as a single person

debate (di-BATE) a discussion between sides

developer (di-VEL-uhp-ur) a person who buys land and builds on it

dynamite (DYE-nuh-mite) a powerful explosive

engulfed (en-GUHLFD) covered completely

etched (ECHD) cut into something

filters (FIL-turz) devices that clean air or water

foreman (FOR-muhn) someone who leads a group of workers

foundation (foun-DAY-shuhn) a solid structure on which a building is built

geometric (jee-uh-MET-rik) made up of lines or shapes

hallowed (HAL-ohd) holy

horizontal (hor-uh-ZON-tuhl) flat; level with the ground

installed (in-STAWLD) put into place for use

landfill (LAND-fill) a hole in the ground used for dumping garbage

lease (LEESS) a rental contract

memorial (muh-MOR-ee-uhl) something that is built to honor a person or an event

officials (uh-FISH-uhlz) people who hold an office or important position

panels (PAN-uhlz) flat pieces of glass or other material

perimeter (puh-RIM-uh-tur) the outside edge of an area

shafts (SHAFTS) long, narrow passages that go straight down

spire (SPIRE) a tall, pointy structure on the top of a building

structure (STRUHK-chur) something that has been built

terrorists (TER-ur-ists) people who use violence to get what they want

tradesmen (TREYDZ-muhn) skilled workers

vertical (VUR-tuh-kuhl) upright or straight up and down

Western Hemisphere (WESS-turn HEM-uhss-fihr) the half of the Earth that includes North America and South America

Bibliography

Blais, Allison, and Lynn Rasic. *A Place of Remembrance: Official Book of the National September 11 Memorial.* Washington, DC: National Geographic (2015).

Darton, Eric. *Divided We Stand: A Biography of the World Trade Center.* New York: Basic Books (2011).

Dupré, Judith. *One World Trade Center: Biography of the Building.* New York: Little, Brown & Company (2016).

Read More

Goldish, Meish. *Ground Zero Dogs (Dog Heroes).* New York: Bearport (2013).

Greene, Jacqueline Dembar. *The 2001 World Trade Center Attack (Code Red).* New York: Bearport (2007).

Kaur, Ramandeep. *One World Trade Center (How Did They Build That?).* New York: Scobre Educational (2015).

Learn More Online

To learn more about One World Trade Center, visit:
www.bearportpublishing.com/AmericanPlaces

Index

About the Author

Meish Goldish has written more than 300 books for children. His book *Colonial Williamsburg* was named a Notable Social Studies Trade Book for Young People in 2017 by the National Council for the Social Studies and the Children's Book Council. He lives in Brooklyn, New York.